71/69

Sweating
Out
the
Winter

*Winner
of the
United
States
Award
of the
International
Poetry
Forum
1968*

Sweating Out the Winter

Poems
by
DAVID
P.
YOUNG

University
of
Pittsburgh
Press

Some of the poems in this volume
first appeared in *Approach*,
The Activist, Carleton Miscellany,
Epoch, kayak, Massachusetts Review,
Paunch, Penny Poems, Tri-Quarterly,
and the 1968 Peace Calendar,
Out of the War Shadow.
"Poem About Hopping" and
"Landscape in Three Lights"
won the *Massachusetts Review*
Tane Award in 1965.

*The International Poetry Forum
and the
University of Pittsburgh Press
acknowledge with gratitude
the assistance
of the Junior League
of Pittsburgh, Inc.,
in making this
book possible.*

To my Wife
and in
Memory of
Newell Ellison

Contents

1

**Late
Summer:
Lake
Erie**

Nearly a year since word of death
Broke off the summer: as if a goddess
You followed respectfully
Should turn and stun you with her look.

We can go back to Old Woman Creek,
Easy canoeing except where lotus
And waterlily choke the way:
Rosemallows massed on the banks, around
Bends, the sudden rise of ducks,
Bluegray bitterns, the silent, ponderous
Heron, the kingfisher escort,
And, under the still, flowering
Surface, death: the orange carp
Crowd toward the killer lake.

I swore I'd write no letters to the dead.
It's only myself I want to tell
Things are about the same. The wind
Still pounds and stumbles around the cottage,
The lake is streaked and rumpled, dead
Fish wash up to the beach, our summer
Is the same, sweet, easily murdered pleasure.
I wade in the supple breakers, I'll
Paddle again on the creek. Now,
This morning, I walk to the road;
All to the south the dazed, hot landscape lies,
Under its piled thunderheads,
Dreaming of love and survival.

The Reapers

Cutting the graveyard grass
was a way to survive our
summer vacations, routine
soon enough, loud slow trips
through a town of headstones,
mausoleums, occasional
solitary grievers.
Funeral processions were short
holidays from work, new graves
were that much less to mow.

So we whiled away our
immortal afternoons, trailing
blue fumes and grass flakes,
dreaming of weekend
girls, beer, drive-ins,
and rode back and forth
on strange machines
above the uninteresting dead,
mowing, endlessly mowing,
emblems
of what we could not understand.

California Street Flying Association

I made my best approach from the southwest
coming in low over fields, windbreaks, Western
Electric, Continental Can, the nunnery,
lower across the golf course, skimming the trees
down Happy Hollow Boulevard
in a roar that froze the hot rods,
so low that, sighting the church,
I had to pull up as well as bank right
in order to crash the house and find
the still attic where twenty years ago
I sit with a cheap old clock between my knees
and try to make it tick and chime again,
climb to ride on the roofpeak, over
puttering neighbors and maples, imagine
rivers flooding between the ridges,
rising steadily against our hill,
the house sliding to the Hollow.

I understand you've had some rain out there.
Well here in the dry forehead of my
July, there's been precipitation too:
the water streams from my wings, across
my windshield, steams on my flying gloves
and mists my instruments as if I'd seen
something in all the fields and rivers of those years
that had to be wept for: a clock, a rooftop boy,
an airplane diving in the rain
toward a white house in Omaha.

5

West of Omaha, Surprised by Fear

Driving into these plains
I tremble and squint, not
wanting to see the terrible white
grain elevators, fertilizer spheres,
the dry stone horizon.

Instead I imagine
bats flipping through aspen groves
in mountain twilight
or the lemon air of certain
harbors and beaches.

But it is no good. The urge
to return, to explore
this spiritual emptiness
invades the dawn gas
and the evening gas.

It means the time has come
to travel the level prairies
of Nebraska and Wyoming;
truck doors swing open inside me
revealing terrible loads.

Desperate I try to recall
pine slopes, red cliffs,
thickets, rockheaps, junkpiles, ravines,
the green teeth of the sea,
but I can't. . . .

Catamounts, stepping delicately,
from the line of mountains
three hundred miles away,
walk with burning eyes
in the flat center of my life.

Summer, A Far-Off War

All afternoon I have driven around
on back roads
thinking of Vietnam.

These huge summer clouds
are like strange moods.
They do not understand their shadows.

This is a country of railroad lilies,
brown, delicate rabbits; how is it
Americans always bring death?

Every few miles a mashed skunk,
some piece of a pheasant;
my windshield stippled with insects. . . .

And I think, Maybe thousands of us
are driving aimlessly
along back roads
hating our war.

Dreams of the Wars

1

When I got to the field they were burning my biplane
why have you given me these titles I yelled
if nothing I say is listened to   feigning great patience
they told me that all information
had to come from the president
the biplane stood by itself
flaring and crackling in the sunset
they stood around and saluted
one of them had an erection
and the smoke crawled away through the poplars
humming a tune

2

sixteen nazis walking through the orchard
have come from shooting the prefect
the prefect smiles they shoot away his hip
they shoot away one half his face he smiles with
the other half they walk back through the orchard
a helmet brushes a lemon blossom
prefect the prefect the prefect
lugers helmets leather and twill

3

the torpedo destroyed a school of porpoises
unpleasant the thrashing and blood in the wake
up on the cliff in the mild evening
we pushed the fat officer over the edge
on the train you told me you had been tortured
I could not speak wrung your hand
put my head in your lap
suddenly wanting sex

4

cold   posters   smoke

another uprising

the red guards of the heart
spilling through the streets

5

barrage balloons in the rain
the stain on the captain's holster
how do you work this mortar
where has the minesweeper gone
this is a gatling gun
a chopper lands in the pasture
we are at war never again

somewhere an eye
is filling with tears
so slowly
it takes hours

Journal

1

I keep hunting myself
In group photographs.
Didn't I used to be simpler,
Like a bare field? Tonight,
Awake in my stiff house, I ask
The emptying parties of the self
Not to linger and chat. Let
The guests wander away
Drunk, in all directions.

2

Brooding and hopeful like this
I am a city darkened for a blitz:

Wires rise from the gardens,
Up is the only direction.
Except for the planes and their burdens.

Everyone waits for day
And the smoke against the sky.

3

This morning, now, I unwrap a package;
Someone has mailed me my father's genitals.
Up in the attic I hear an ocarina.

I am suddenly peopled by ancient
Bureaucrat-poets. Smiling politely,
They tuck up their robes to cross my threshold.

And the Angel of Death, too! Apollyon.
He stands out back, by my garage,
Swinging his great horse-pistol in the rain.

4

Sometimes the self is cracked and peeled.
It's twilight here. It's spring.
The moon is new and narrow,
The air is pure; things
Belong. This empty field
Dreams of the farm in every furrow
As the body dreams the mind,
The windmill dreams the wind.

Three Chrysanthemum Poems

1

I am looking down at the garden
Of the house in Minneapolis,
Ignoring the loved voices
Calling from darker rooms. Somehow,
I squeeze through the sunporch window,
Spread like a cloud above the yard,
And explode, showering the garden.

Absorbed, countrified,
Loam, stem, petal and weed,
I am not I. My name
Is flower beside the yard,
Gold in the hot garden;
Call me chrysanthemum.

2

Time of the wild
Chrysanthemum: elsewhere,
At noon on a headland
Above a gleaming ocean
A Chinese sentry
Drunk on sorghum brandy
Plants a flower in his rifle
Barrel, raises it, fires
At the nearest star.

3

An old black biplane
Hangs in the air, mysterious
Above our sun-flecked town.
A man crawls on the wing, his
Hair stirred by the wind,
Reaching out his hand.

The plane floats away, struts
Quivering in the still noon,
Like a leaf or a dazed bat.
It will only land when
The sun turns chrysanthemum,
A stiff, mad ornament.

To Say What Time Is

1

Up near Tincup Pass,
Close to the top,
We flushed a spruce grouse,
A foolhen. The soft explosion
Broke up the afternoon.

2

Sometimes I touch your face
And sense the bone beneath,
Flaring to make the cheek,
A hard, last
Syllable.

3

The ghost town was inhabited
By morose summer vacationers.
We never saw one close.
At a distance, faces in broken windows,
They had a preoccupied air.

4

Once, on a beach stroll
We found scribbles of blood
Leading into the water.

We had just missed seeing
Some staggering king.

5

Remember the fox? A dark
Rust shape among the rocks.
He was gone when we arrived
And there was a rank patch of smell,
An afterthought.

6

The rain does its work;
The town smells like a lake.
For a long time now,
Behind doors, beyond trees,
Dark water has been rising.

August at the Lake

Shall we sit here some more
On old lawnchairs, while the wind
Settles across our fingers?

Maybe the purple martins
Have already reached the tropics;

But we aren't migratory birds.
We have too much to pack.

So we sit here, our faces
Working, while the red evening
Climbs the fence and is gone.

Two
for
the
Hampton
Institute

*(Based on
photographs
from the
Hampton Album,
taken by
Frances B.
Johnston, 1900.)*

1

The class is judging swine.

We are afraid that the mud
Will soil their grandmother dresses
And union soldier uniforms.

The teacher, who looks like a chauffeur,
Points to the loafing pigs
And the class follows his gaze,

But a turn-of-the-century swine
Looks out from under his ears
In our direction.

"This beautiful dream," he says. . . .
Old leaves blow past.
A windmill spins in the distance.

2

The history class on the cliff
Inspects the great black cannon.
An iron whale in the sunlight,
It can fire into the sea.

The tough grass holds our shadow
As we step back to view
The cluster of dark learners
Posed in the line of fire.

In the background the sea remains
The sea, immense and restless.
There are no thoughts in the air;
Impossibly pale: the sky

Like an Old Rite in Delaware

Drunk on gin, summer, and their
Underlying terror, they were
Out in the dark chasing
Lightning bugs.

A woman stumbled and lay
In the wet grass, chuckling.
A man came by and took her.
Around their breathless thrashing,
Rising and falling like rootless stars,
The fireflies.

Colloquy for a Mountain

A lonely country? It's not the trucks
Whining all night through rain, it's not
Ten empty fields where a meadowlark
Calls to himself. What's this but
Acceptable solitude? And who'd
Trade it for any multitude?

    Well, what about old abandoned
    Mineshafts, factories, collapsing shacks,
    Ghost towns drying in the empty mind
    Of the wind, the traces of track
    On railroad barrows, and the deep
    Empty quarries, echoless in sleep?

It's true that we resent
Our ruins, segregate our ghosts,
Raze ageing buildings or patch up their fronts
To stop the talk about the past.
The wind scrabbles through the mountain pass,
The white boat rots in the forage grass.

    It's not just restlessness that makes
    Us lie about forebears and invent
    A storybook history, forsake
    Whole towns and wander off to hunt
    Fountains and Lodestones in the wilderness,
    The deadly hug of the whore Success.

Well, since you must list and edify,
You can add this to your concoction:
In parts of Ohio, when you die,
They bury you, then hold an auction.
You can cremate me when I go
And scatter me over Toledo.

No morals, then, I don't care.
I'd rather recall a day I had
Once in Vermont when I found an obscure
And almost forgotten logging road.
I followed it all one afternoon
And I don't believe I was alone.

Oh Salmon-colored Edsel, Run Us Down

1

Always in autumn you cannot say what you mean.
Your eyes grow heavy, your head rolls.
You make a sound like an airplane
too high to see.

2

An insurance man is falling asleep at the wheel.
Death is all he wants:
shot down by drunken hunters,
stuffed and set up, a pumpkin man,
in some Slav's yard.

And the housewife, in her sad scarf:
she wants to lie in the leaves
among blackening apples and walnuts,
she wants the leaves heaped up, frost-glazed,
she wants to be forgotten.

We are all heavy with this dark tug;
the fireman dreams himself in flames,
the teacher is dismembered by his class,
the farmer is crucified on his windmill.

We are sick of vicarious death; we want the real thing.
Our eyelids are carved of oak and our hands
shake when we try to use them.

3

Sunday morning at the Discount Center,
entrance to the kingdom of the dead.

They have a new machine here.
Put a quarter in this large white horse,
and he'll paw you to death.

4

Sometime in November it starts to snow,
softly, from gunblue clouds.

We light lamps early and build fires.
Blood rises in us again,
a naked dancer, slowly plunging
forward, head down,
shaking and singing.

2

The Man Who Swallowed a Bird

Happened when he was yawning.
A black or scarlet bird went down his throat
And disappeared, and at the time
He only looked foolish, belched a feather;
The change took time.

But when we saw him again in the
Half-dusk of a summer evening
He was a different man. His eyes
Glittered and his brown hands
Lived in the air like swallows;
Knowledge of season lit his face
But he seemed restless. What he said
Almost made sense, but from a distance:

> Once I swallowed a bird,
> Felt like a cage at first, but now
> Sometimes my flesh flutters and I think
> I could go mad for joy.

In the fall he vanished. South
Some said, others said dead. Jokes
About metamorphosis were made. Nonetheless,
Some of us hear odd songs.
                              Suppose
You press your ear against the morning air,
Above and on your left you might
Hear music that implies without a word
A world where a man can absorb a bird.

More about Skills

I saw myself talking
At a distance, hands busy

With the air: scooping it,
Shaping it, drawing it out,

And brushing it away,
A story of hands and arms.

The words were lost like smoke
But the gestures were ancient

Signs that I took to say:
How do we know our medium

Except we divide it
With our hands, breaking its bread,

Pouring its thin wine. Here
Is a batch I have gathered,

Before it disperses, inspect
It, sift and caress it,

Carry it weightless on your
Wrists, your unmapped palms,

Drink it, spring in the blood,
Return it in smoky words,

Words that beget gestures,
Gestures assembling the air.

Landscape with a Hunt

In the poised, bright picture the entire hunt
Is held and ordered for inspection. The hounds
Respectfully run without moving toward the deep
Recesses of the forest and the great groomed

Horses prance and sidle in becoming attitudes
That can be counted on not to alter. Likewise
Their riders, patient in finery, do not bridle
At having been locked, for art's sake, into place.

But to turn the eye away is perhaps to allow
The mind's horn to release the scene
And send the hunt packing. Oh then the confusion
Sets in. All's movement and flash, too much to watch

Or too much to bear though the terrible moment
Is brief. The hounds bound yapping into the far
Forest, the horses wheel and crash off with their
Riders hollering, and the whole fine scene

Dwindles to distant horns and yelps and then
Goes utterly quiet. The glazed and anxious eye
Can turn to the picture again to be reassured,
But the mind is bereft. That hunt will not return.

Will Tarzan Swing in Time

Will Tarzan swing in time
down on his tall vine
to knock the nasty priest
(whose knife is at the breast
of Jane, while Boy lies stunned
where the python has him pinned)
into the muddy river
where crocodiles slaver
lying in wait?
Can we count on that?

And will his friend the gallant
but badly injured elephant
overtake the foul explorer
(fleeing just now in terror)
who stole the Sacred Ruby
and step on the big booby?
Only in the movie.
Can the monkeys bear to look?
Only in the book.

That's all you need to know
reader, now please don't go
asking if nature imitates art.
See what you'd start:
explorer finds ruby is glass,
Jane is a bloody mess,
elephant creeps off to die,
python swallows Boy,
and Tarzan runs back up his vine,
more like an ape than a man.

Segal

The girl who sits on the bed
facing the window while her lover sleeps

leans, hands on the mattress, into
a blue, enormously late, light

her arms, face, breasts all turning
blue while she thinks about nothing

but simply carries her sorrow
and is unconscious of her beauty

while in the room where the sculptor
has put her, the light comes slowly

back to bright, as her white skin
grows whiter, her flesh more solid,

she, her lover, the bed, unstained
by color or darkness, polar, thick,

as if the light could take us unaware
when we knew least that we were what

we hoped we'd be, calm and intact;
as if the light could give us what we lacked.

Putting
It
Mildly

Into the uproar of April emerged Mr. Marblearch,
Ready again to be well aware of the weather,
For a normal informal part in the burgeoning season's
Annual matters of magnitude.

Like a cat encountering cream he encountered the colors
And tapped his cigar so as not to endanger the flowers;
He paused in thought by a solemn and wild forsythia,
Fancies assailing his head.

"This sun," Mr. Marblearch said, "is enlarged
Like the oldest thought enjoying its newest form
In an epochal fashion. Ahem. It is like a sublime
Balloon that will never burst.

"Furthermore," he went on, beneath a magnolia,
"To have a sky in one's head, a bush in the breast,
Is to partake of the pattern, the bee and the tree
Being in season."

Marblearch colored in the season's din
With the whole magnolia, alive on the grass
In the role of forsythia, feeling the morning sun's
Ideas hot on his face.

in memory of Wallace Stevens

The Small-Town Poets

I

There is so much green in summer
That the town sinks through water,
A mottled Atlantis, where you might stroll
On a brick street, some leaky evening
And see above you a black whale
Nosing and browsing
Among the caverns of the trees.

Someone has to take notes
So we have small-town poets.

They all teach at the college,
They all have wives and children.
Shy, groomed, inclined to plumpness,
They're nothing much to look at;
Most of their lives are out of sight
Like the inside of a lake,
The reaches of a coalmine.

And what they bring to the surface
Is apt to make you nervous.

2

By day the old houses are reassuring
But at night
Nothing is blacker
Than the glass of the high, narrow windows.

Owls drift across
Lawns, through garden updrafts,
Time gapes like a nightbloom
Houses wobble and cloud
And U-boats begin to move
Above the sidewalks in the hum of sleep.

The poets sleep loose
Or lie awake and watch
The dreams come booming.

One snaps up, 2 a.m.
With a vision of black and white
Mountains, wind, mist,
And dead men with beards
Sprawled in the snow.
He trots to his desk to jot them down.

One dreams, when his son is born
That his streamlined plastic car
Is becoming his father's old
Studebaker, the huge rear window
Shrinking, dividing.

Another stands on his porch
Facing old presences:
Ancestor trees
Rise crackling in the fields and streets
And a mastodon, unruffled by his
Steady dying, drinks from a pool
And walks away through the bakery.

3

Even in daylight
They have it rough with reality:

During a walk to the store
A rough beast goes by
In a highly polished car.

In the schoolyard booted gnomes
Climb and scream on the swings.

A chicken as big as a kitchen.
The faces of adolescents.

Waves of hate from South America
Blowing down Main Street an hour after dawn.

Tornadoes south of town.

Inside even some of the children
An iron helmet, a uniform.

It may be the morning stars
Chorus together. It's also true
The planets cry out to one another
Lonely, dazed, in their terrible circling.

4

They live, like the local florist,
At the edge of every ceremony
Handling the tall, cold roses.

Orpheus, for example, seen
Walking into the funeral home.
He may emerge.
Something capable survives
Almost confident among
The rotted imaginations,
Something almost capable
Of intervening in your life,
A mooncalf in a supermart
An ancestor delivering mail
The right light on a Wednesday morning:
I live in this mild sprawl, you shall say,
Seize me by the hand, lead where you will!
I would be one with the edge of town, the garden,
The wren, the stone, the tank-town poet,
The one-night-stand musician.

5

A last glance at these chaps:
On a giant Sunday afternoon
They charter a small plane
To take them to where they can
Stare down at their lives.

They crowd in the cockpit
With cameras, notebooks,
Useless binoculars;
Pegasus roars and taxis
Out of a cloud of dust,
Bumps on its runway, skips,
And soars up into morning. . . .
Free of the earth's
Litter of dreams
They grin. They are the sun.
The town turns into a poem.
They have forgotten why they came.

Let them stay there a bit
In the speechless mind of the wind,
Everything safe on the ground,
The poets circling.

A Still from an Old Film

The eagle carries the baby
Far over hills and water.

It seems a safe disaster:
The baby has folded its hands
And looks composed: below
Its ample lace-rimmed gown
Its large legs dangle down
Clad in black shoes and socks
Above the hills and water.

I tack the grainy still
To my wall. It makes me smile,
Envying them their orbit
In a lost and windless day
Above what we become:
A stretch of hills and water.

3

Poem about Hopping

Rabbits in Alabama hop
into clumps of Syrian grass
to nibble the stalks, thinking of
sorghum, hardly noticing autumn.

Along the Great Divide the bighorn
sheep hop casually from rock to
rock in the wind and glare, seriously
considering leaping silver rivers, as

salmon in crazy waters jump
upstream for love—oh it's
a nervous country. When you
walk through stubble, the hub

of a wheel with grasshopper
spokes, or sit over bowls of excited
cereal, what can you say to your heart
but, Down sir, down sir, down?

Evasions

1

Late afternoon; the light
Slides down the bricks.
There is no wind or sound.
The day forgets its way.
Nothing but distance; now,
Down at the farther
End of the mind, a farmer
Douses the lamp and climbs
The narrow stairs to sleep.

All night, under the window,
A horse gallops in the pasture.

2

Lie down, your mind stands up,
Listening.
Close your eyes, you see
The faces of madmen
Floating below, eyes rolling
Just beyond understanding.

At the door to the pasture
Stands your father
Holding his dark brain
Cupped in his hands. The weather
Has brought you back together.

3

Crackpot snapshots!
Coon, bricks, stars,
Beast in the pasture.
Poets don't have to be
Told they are liars.
Once more, word-sponge,

You wait. For yourself
To be whole,
Head back on the body,
True poem, the long moment,
A moose, coming slowly through soaked grass
In the rising light.

4

The only sound in this room
Is the air-conditioner's hum

But simply to close my eyes
Is to smell those pewter skies.

And stand like a patient hunter
In the stripped fields of winter

Remembering the heat
And the high, wet wheat

The etchings of the sun
And all the people gone.

Didn't I say the weather
Would gather me back together?

Was it at Halloween
I carved my face, scooped my brain?

A seedy, saffron pumpkin,
Lined with the wind, I grin.

On Neglecting to Baptize a Child

Now that our son is come,
    The house turns mythic:
Milk drips from the eaves,
    Leaves grow in the attic.

At dusk great kings drift in
    To serenade us.
The plumbing drums; like priests
    The radiators hiss.

Christmas is near; we three
    Enact in parody,
Like figures in a crèche,
    Scenes of nativity.

It's not the same, thank God,
    It's simpler mystery.
What do we know, all told,
    Of immortality?

Have we deceived our friends
    Having no christening?
We feel, root, branch, and bud,
    Our lives turn evergreen.

Two Renewal Poems

1 *The Line*

What weather is this?
My body is heavy, real; it walks
Out of the house, into the wind.
My small son watches from the window;
I wave and walk away.
A bluejay stalls
Above a spruce. My
Forehead touches the cold glass.
My father waves
And walks away.

2 *The Circle*

Driving across Iowa
in the corn-green light, you
sometimes come across
between the road and pasture
a knee-high gush of water
from a deep artesian well
rising and tumbling into itself
in the raw sun, cold and sweet.

You stand at the center of summer,
your life rising and falling.

Take a tin can from the fencepost.
Drink.

Landscape in Three Lights

Under the round clouds
the flowers lean and yawn
stiff to the wind; shreds
of plumblossom stain
one corner of lawn. Down
farther a rabbit ponders
the scene, his small, drawn
face alert for intruders.

They come. All afternoon
in the dispersing light
groups of people in fine
clothes wander and chat;
they gesture, laugh, croquet
balls tick, ice chinks, but turn
where they will, the rising night
surrounds their paper lanterns.

It is the past, this dark.
The people disappear, their
murmuring grows berserk
in the wind. And what's left here?
Somebody's drunk ancestor
walking home to the moon
through the stubble corn, past care,
humming an old tune.

Nineteen Sixty-three

The year the president was killed
Was the same my friend was shot
On a Washington street one night
For his white skin and wallet.

What we can't bear we bury.
I got so I thought I could
Stand the abruptness if only
There were some final word.

But when he returned in a dream
Dying and white like Gracchus,
And there was a chance to explain,
We were both shy and speechless.

Then I grew light with wonder
Watching beside the bed,
My stubbornness fell away
For I thought I understood

That he wouldn't elect to live
Here at the end of the myth
If he could, and I smiled and said
"You're the President of Death."

Sweating Out the Winter

Like an old pot on the stove
My head simmers and rattles.
Outside, beyond the window,
A cloud of steam from the dryer
Rises through steadily falling snow.

In the warm sack of my body
I drowse, losing the past.

The land remembers its huge snows,
The death of animals
(Haybales dropped
for the stiffening cattle).

The water, its skin turned
Brittle as birdbones by the wind,
Remembers summer like a soft,
Blowing steam.

My palms are wet. Blinking,
I lean toward the window.

Forest and wastes.
Blank white lakes.

In the distance a city
Steams and smokes on the cold plain
Under gray and ivory clouds.
I close my eyes. More wastes!
Massed ice, the flecked dome
Of father Eisenhower! The soft
Groans of freezing hoboes (bodies
that won't be found until the thaw),
Speeches for reform, crowds,
Cries and thuds at the line of scrimmage.

And quiet. The noiseless
Snowing, small women asleep
In white and gilt bedrooms,
The president's coffin, centered
In the rotunda, below the dome,
The Texaco station on the corner
Where Negroes linger.

Come north, hums the wind
Off the ice cap. In vast white wastes
The caribou survive.
To know how to store
Warmth! In his skin boat
The eskimo sets out, a precarious
Floating. I reach out.
The pane clouds at my touch and then
Begins to clear.

COLOPHON

The poems in this book are set in the Linotype version of Times Roman, a typeface first designed for the *London Times*. Its classic modern style and extreme readability soon made it a popular typeface for books as well, and today it is a mainstay of the printers' art. The presswork is directly from the type, on Warren's Olde Style antique wove paper, by Heritage Printers, Inc. The design is by Gary Gore.

PITT POETRY SERIES